Disney's Beauty and the Beast

A POSTCARD BOOK™

RUNNING PRESS • PHILADELPHIA, PENNSYLVANIA

Copyright © 1992 The Walt Disney Company

All rights reserved under the Pan-American and International Copyright Conventions. This book may not be reproduced in whole or in part in any form or by any means, electronic or mechanical, including photocopying, recording, or by any information storage and retrieval system now known or hereafter invented, without written permission from the publisher.

Canadian representatives: General Publishing Co., Ltd., 30 Lesmill Road, Don Mills, Ontario M3B 2T6. International representatives: Worldwide Media Services, Inc., 30 Montgomery Street, Jersey City, New Jersey 07302.

9 8 7 6 5 4
The digit on the right indicates the number of this printing.

ISBN 1-56138-162-4
Cover design by Toby Schmidt
Interior design by Jacqueline Spadaro
Typography: Goudy Oldstyle by Commcor Communications, Philadelphia, Pennsylvania
Printed and bound in the United States by Philadelphia Press.

This book may be ordered by mail from the publisher. Please add $2.50 for postage and handling. *But try your bookstore first!* Running Press Book Publishers, 125 South Twenty-second Street, Philadelphia, Pennsylvania 19103

"Who could ever learn to love a beast?" With this age-old question, Disney's 30th full-length animated feature film begins. *Beauty and the Beast* tells the story of a courageous young woman and her encounter with a violent-tempered, enchanted beast—an encounter that changes both of them forever.

Walt Disney Pictures transformed the familiar fairy tale into the most ambitious animated feature ever brought to the screen. The film stars a varied cast of characters, including the angry but vulnerable Beast; Belle, the beautiful, strong-willed heroine; and a supporting cast of animated inanimate objects—Lumiere, the passionate French candlestick; Cogsworth, the uptight English clock; and Mrs. Potts, the teakettle with the bubbling personality.

This enduring romantic adventure presented a 3½-year

challenge to Disney's feature animation staff. Together, nearly 600 talented animators, artists, and technicians produced more than a million drawings and thousands of meticulously colored frames of film. Character animation was done completely by hand, and the animation team also used innovative computer-generated imagery to create the fully-dimensional backgrounds that give the film its unusual visual depth.

Beauty and the Beast, the first animated feature to be nominated for Best Picture by the Academy of Motion Picture Arts and Sciences, was honored with two Oscars—for Best Original Score and Best Song. But, like beauty, acclaim is only skin-deep. It is the film's engaging characters, dramatic story line, and soaring musical score that captivate us.

Disney's answer to the eternal question, "Who could ever learn to love a beast?" is a simple one.

We all can.

Once upon a time in a faraway land a young prince lived in a shining castle.

Disney's **Beauty** and the **Beast** A Postcard Book™ Running Press Book Publishers
© Disney

Belle begins her day with a trip to town.

Disney's Beauty and the Beast A Postcard Book™ Running Press Book Publishers
© Disney

Belle dreams of a more adventurous life.

Disney's **Beauty** and the **Beast**   A Postcard Book™   Running Press Book Publishers
© Disney

Gaston tells Belle he's more important than books.

Disney's **Beauty** and the **Beast** A Postcard Book™ Running Press Book Publishers
© Disney

Belle and Maurice watch Maurice's invention chop wood.

Disney's Beauty and the Beast   A Postcard Book™   Running Press Book Publishers
© Disney

As he sets out for the fair, Maurice waves goodbye to Belle.

Disney's **Beauty** and the **Beast**   A Postcard Book™   Running Press Book Publishers
© Disney

Belle dreams of far-off places.

Disney's **Beauty** and the **Beast**   A Postcard Book™   Running Press Book Publishers
© Disney

Gaston boasts about his own greatness.

Disney's **Beauty** and the **Beast** A Postcard Book™ Running Press Book Publishers
© Disney

An enchanted vase offers Belle a flower.

Disney's **Beauty** and the **Beast** A Postcard Book™ Running Press Book Publishers
© Disney

Lumiere and the enchanted objects present a feast and invite Belle to "Be Our Guest."

Disney's Beauty and the Beast A Postcard Book™ Running Press Book Publishers
© Disney

The Beast discovers Belle in the forbidden West Wing.

Disney's *Beauty and the Beast* A Postcard Book™ Running Press Book Publishers
© Disney

Belle and Philippe are cornered by vicious wolves.

Disney's **Beauty** and the **Beast** A Postcard Book™ Running Press Book Publishers
© Disney

Mrs. Potts admonishes her son, Chip.

Disney's **Beauty** and the **Beast**　A Postcard Book™　Running Press Book Publishers
© Disney

During breakfast, Belle and the Beast toast one another.

Disney's **Beauty** and the **Beast** A Postcard Book™   Running Press Book Publishers
© Disney

Belle teaches the Beast to feed the birds.

Disney's **Beauty** and the **Beast**   A Postcard Book™   Running Press Book Publishers
© Disney

Belle sees the Beast in a new light.

Disney's Beauty and the Beast A Postcard Book™ Running Press Book Publishers
© Disney

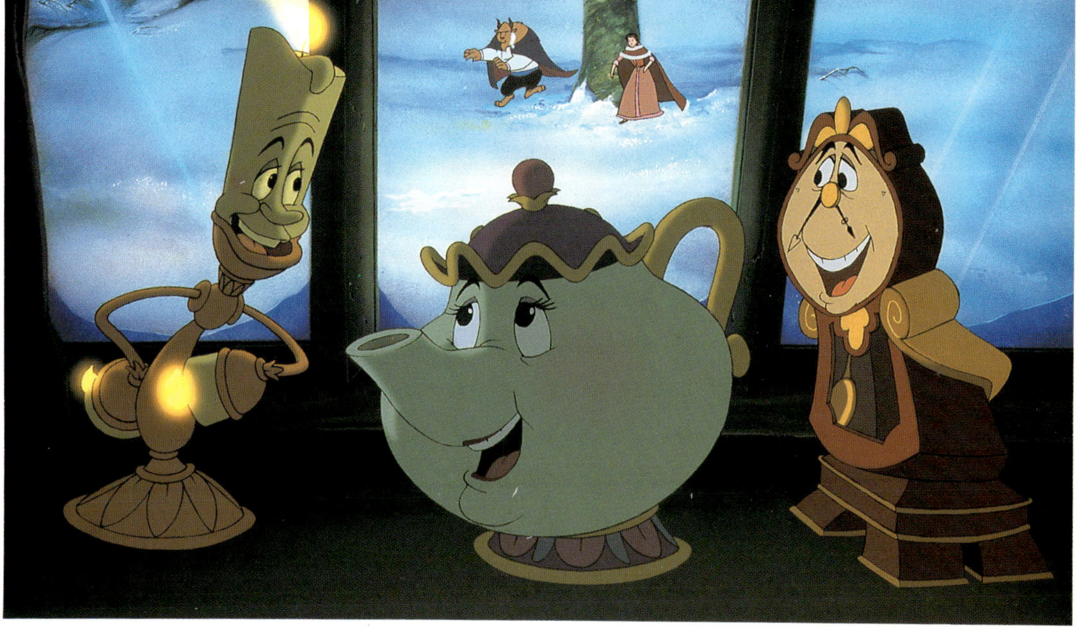

Lumiere, Mrs. Potts, and Cogsworth hope that the budding friendship of Belle and the Beast will break the spell.

Disney's **Beauty** and the **Beast** A Postcard Book™ Running Press Book Publishers
© Disney

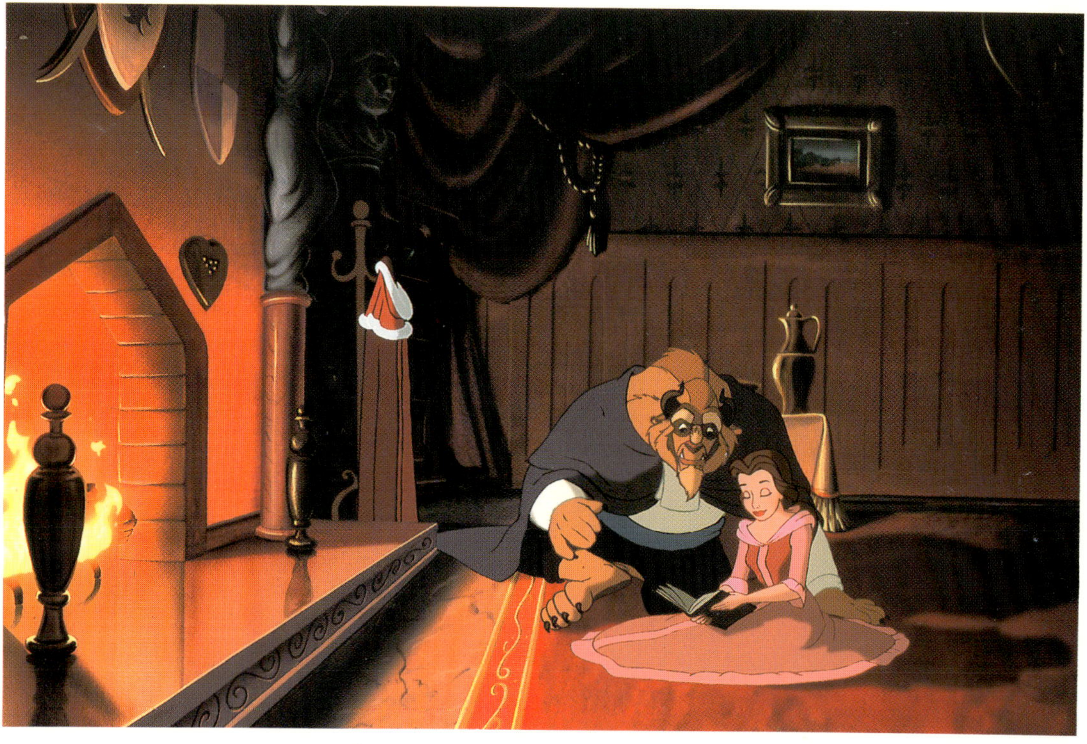

The Beast and Belle read together.

Beauty and the **Beast** A Postcard Book™ Running Press Book Publishers
Disney's
© Disney

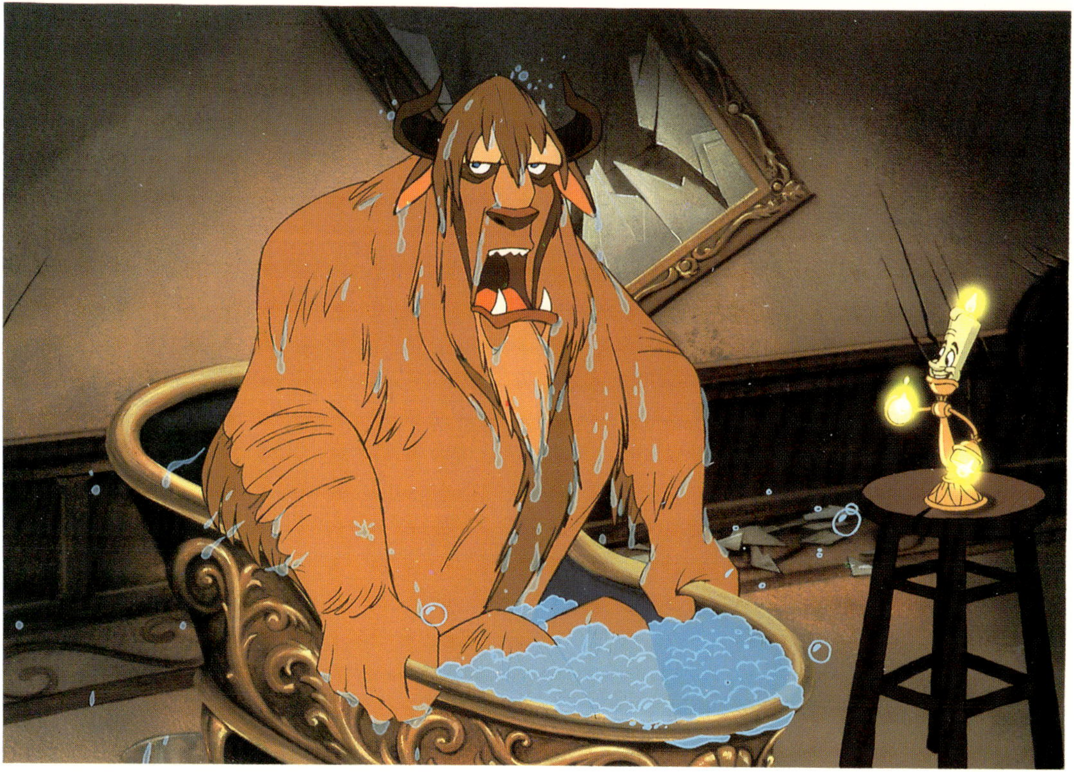

Before dressing for dinner, the Beast bathes.

Disney's *Beauty and the Beast* A Postcard Book™ Running Press Book Publishers
© Disney

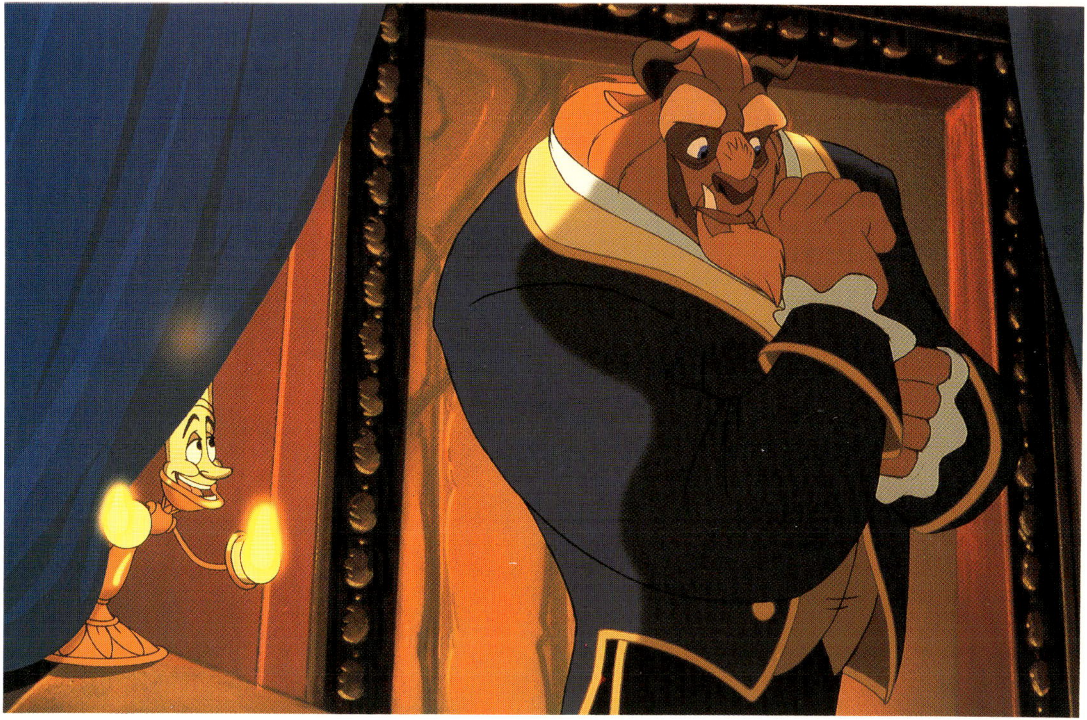

Lumiere coaches the Beast in matters of the heart.

Disney's *Beauty and the Beast* A Postcard Book™ Running Press Book Publishers
© Disney

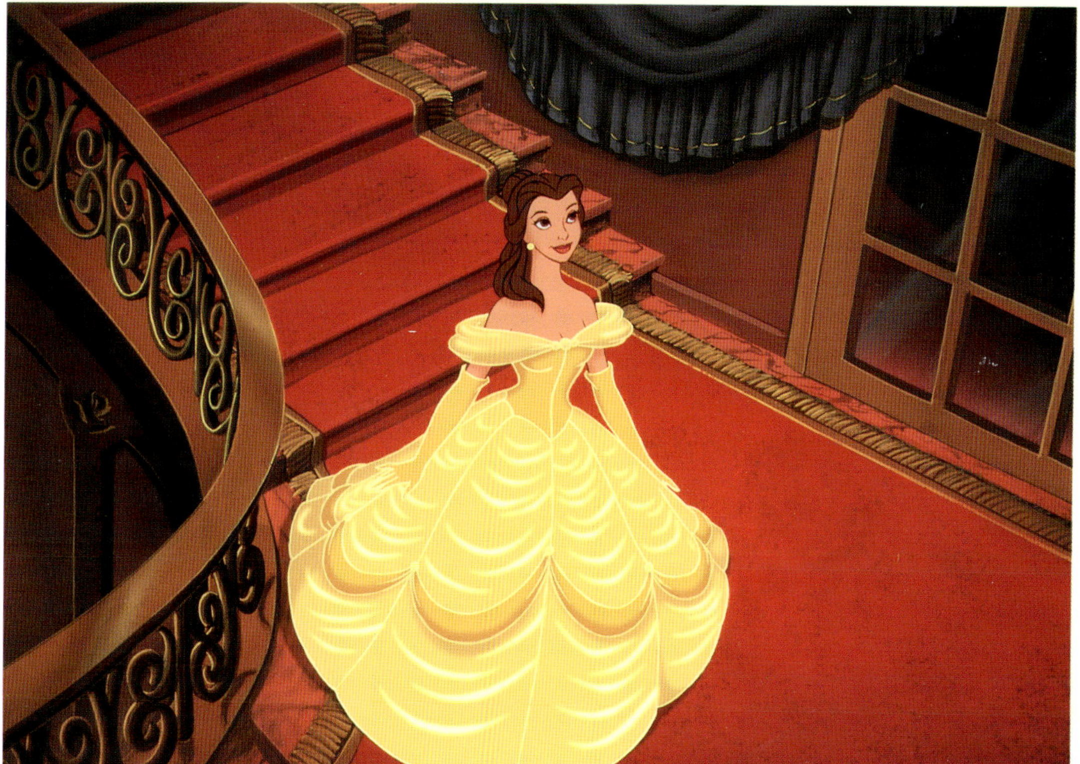

Belle waits for the Beast to escort her to dinner.

Disney's Beauty and the Beast A Postcard Book™ Running Press Book Publishers
© Disney

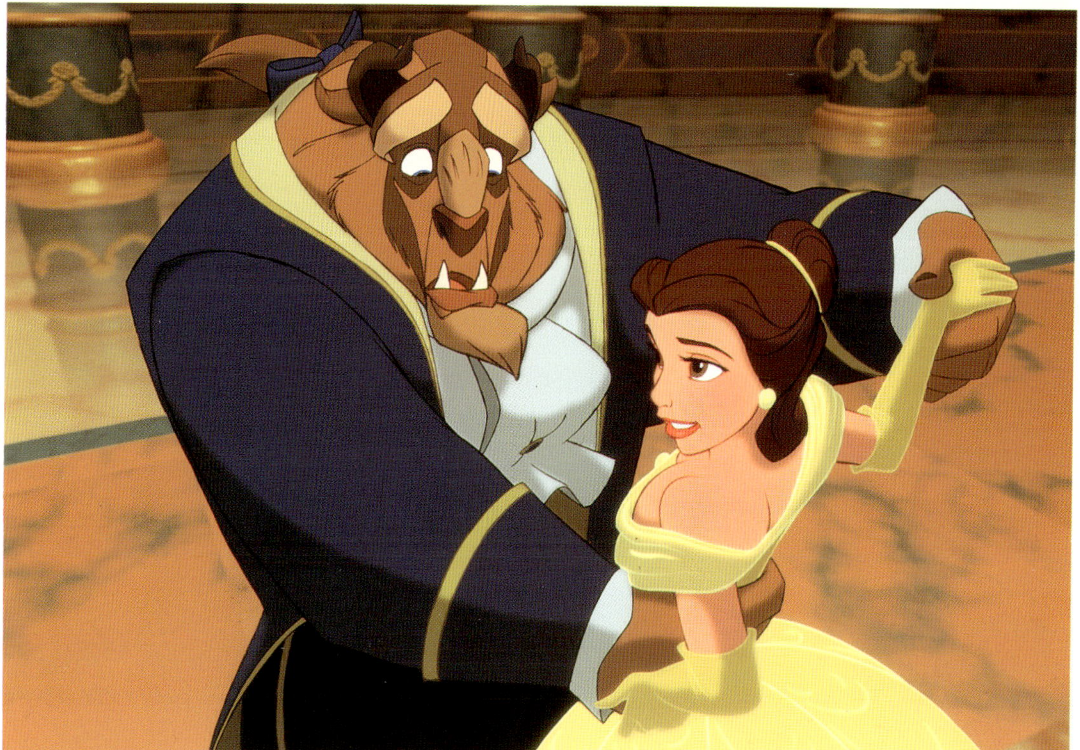

Belle and the Beast dance in the ballroom of the Beast's castle.

Disney's **Beauty** and the **Beast** A Postcard Book™ Running Press Book Publishers
© Disney

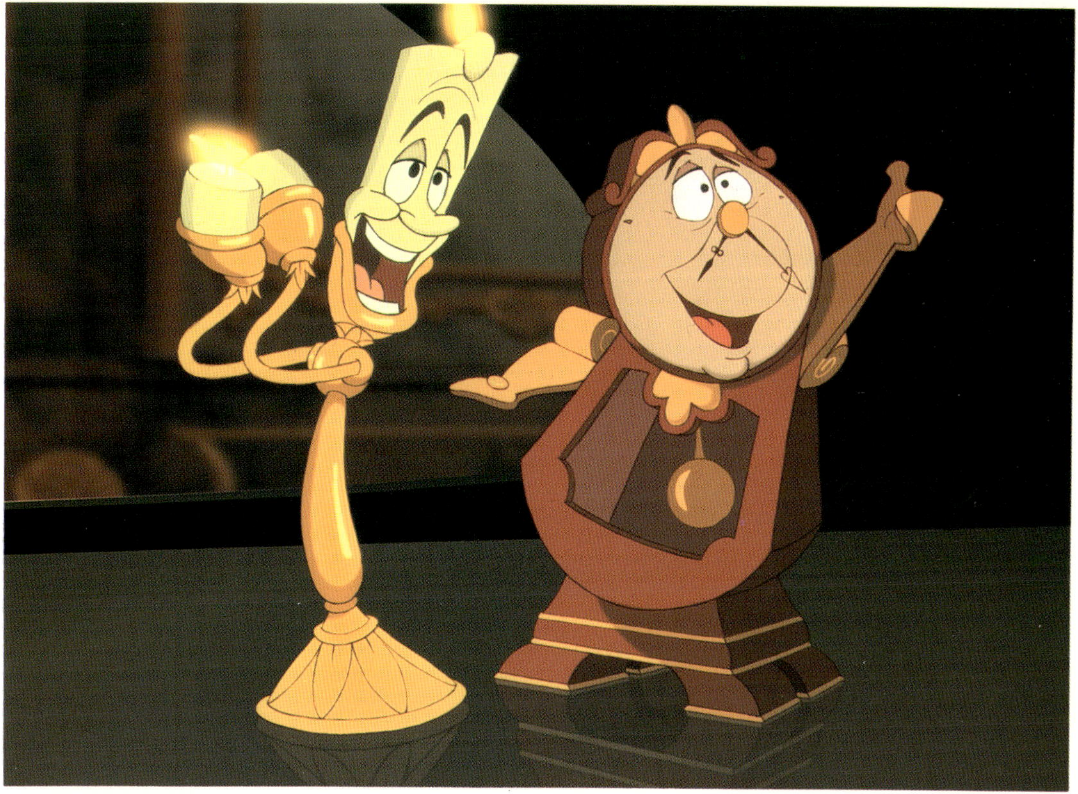

Cogsworth and Lumiere cheer as Belle and the Beast dance.

Disney's Beauty and the Beast A Postcard Book™ Running Press Book Publishers
© Disney

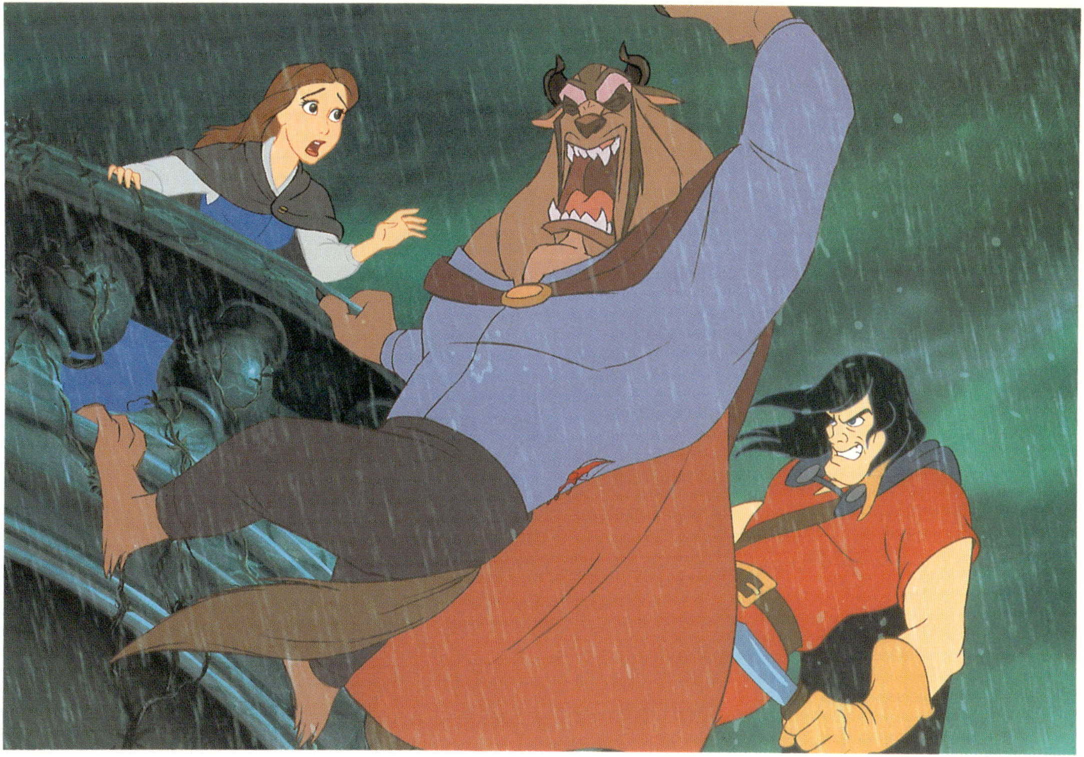

Gaston stabs the Beast in the back.

Disney's Beauty and the Beast   A Postcard Book™   Running Press Book Publishers
© Disney

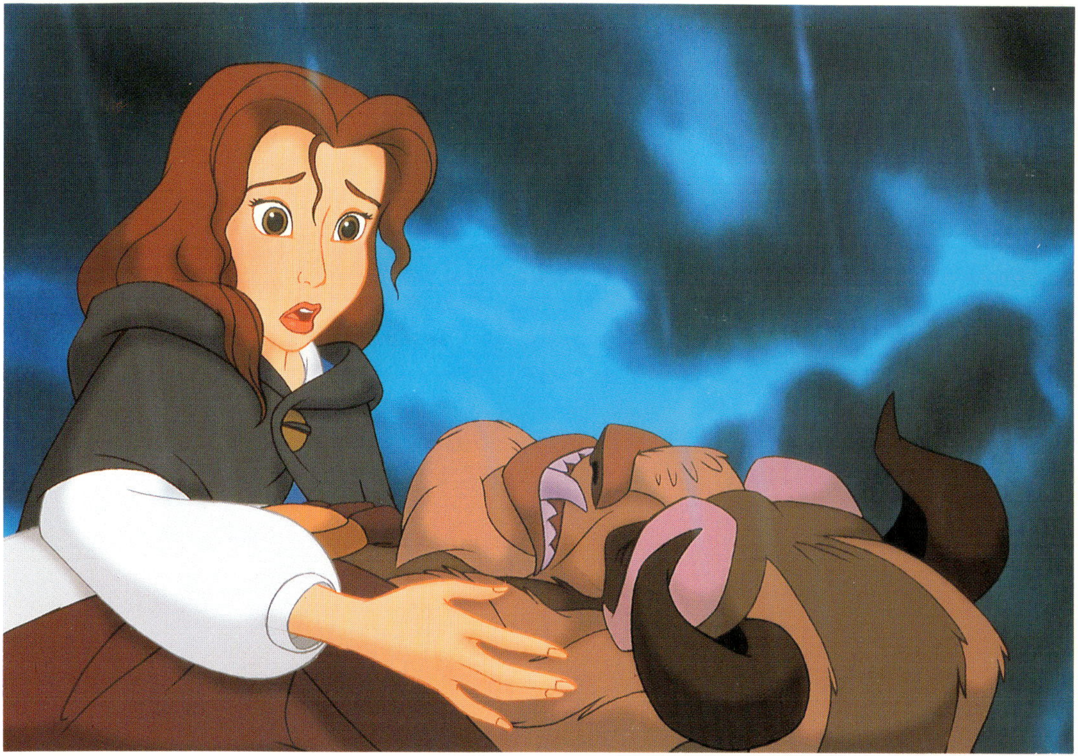

Belle confesses her love for the wounded Beast.

Disney's Beauty and the Beast   A Postcard Book™   Running Press Book Publishers
© Disney

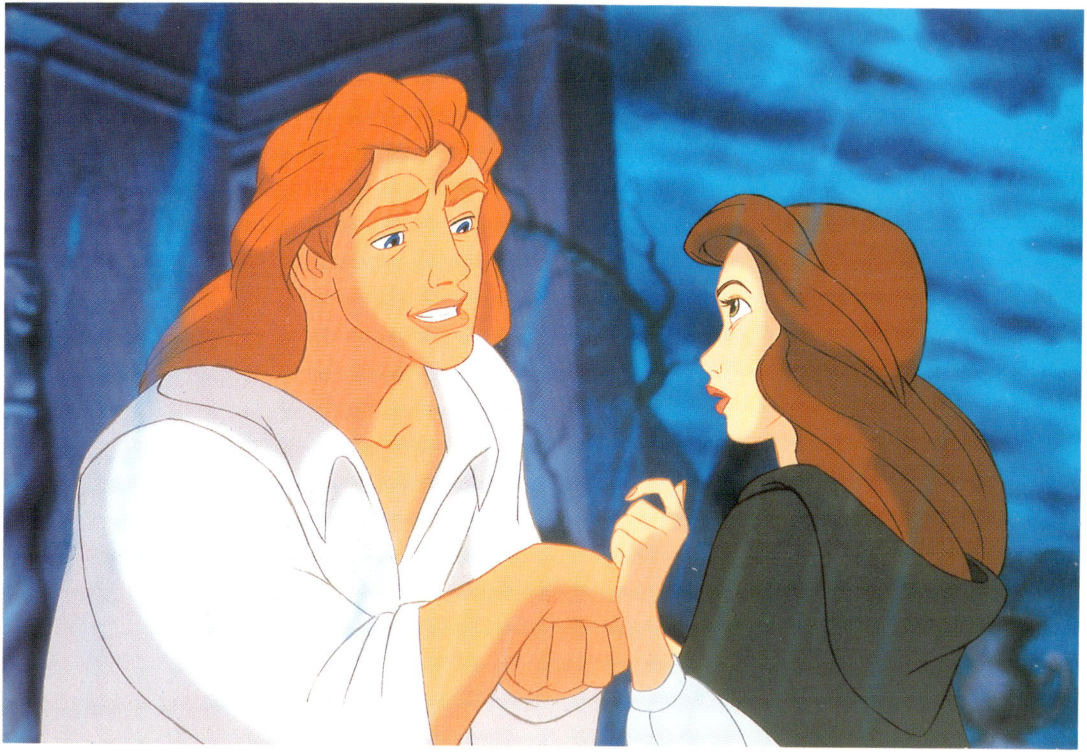

The Prince convinces Belle that he is the Beast transformed.

Disney's Beauty and the Beast © Disney   A Postcard Book™   Running Press Book Publishers

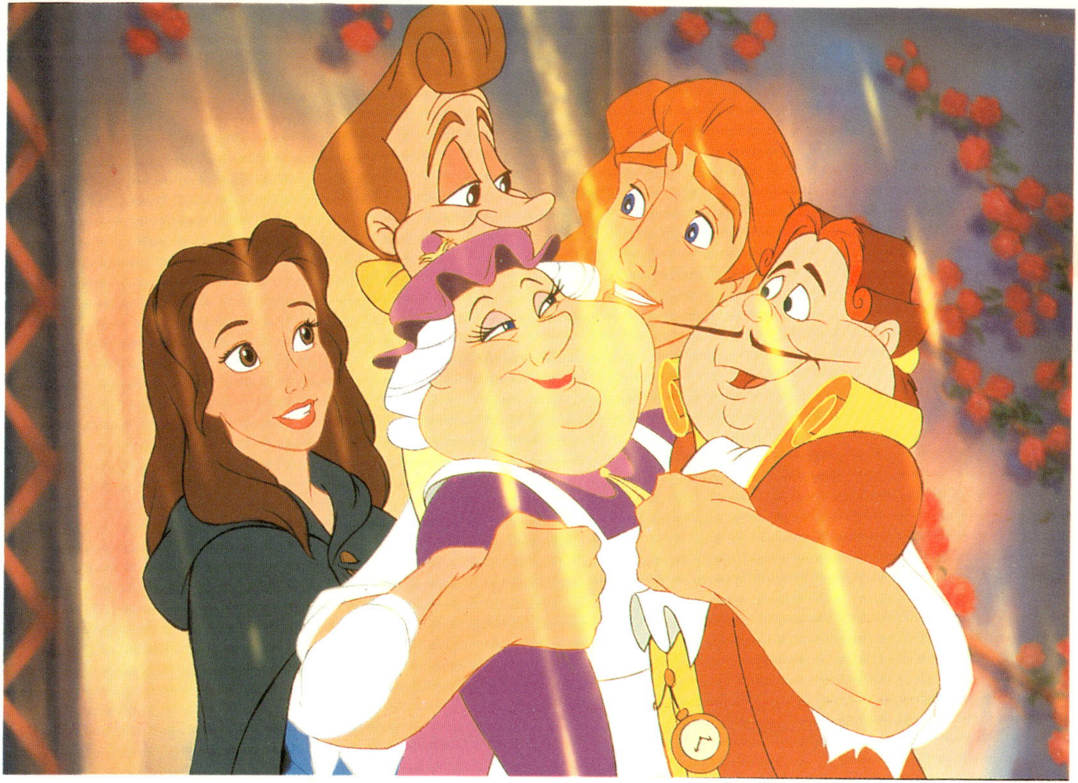

After the transformation of the Beast, Belle watches as the Prince, Cogsworth, Mrs. Potts, and Lumiere reunite.

Disney's Beauty and the Beast A Postcard Book™ Running Press Book Publishers
© Disney

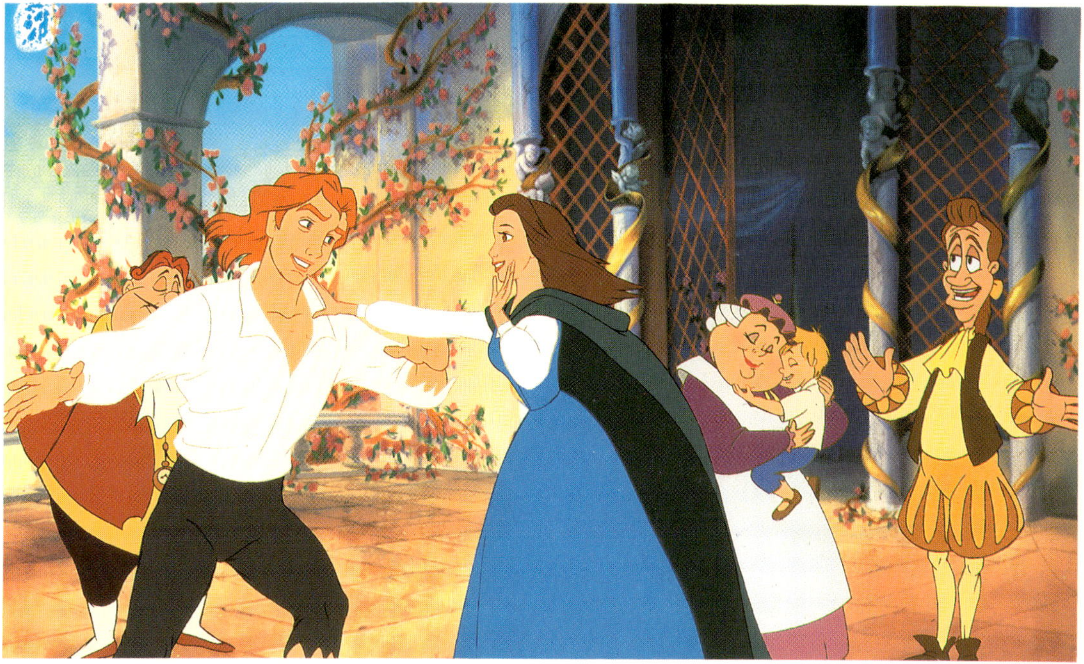

Belle and the Prince embrace.

Disney's Beauty and the Beast A Postcard Book™ Running Press Book Publishers
© Disney

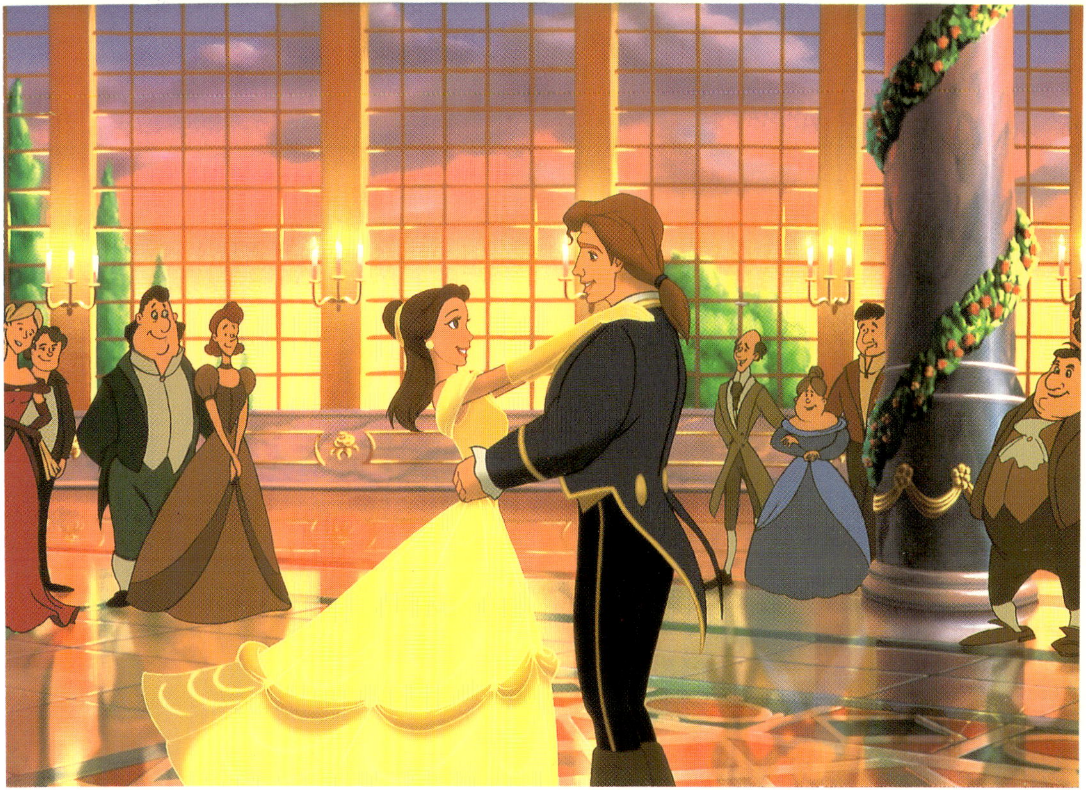

Belle and the Prince dance.

Disney's Beauty and the Beast A Postcard Book™ Running Press Book Publishers
© Disney